OTHER BOOKS BY HELEN EXLEY:

Over 60s' Jokes	Cat Jokes
Over 70s' Jokes	365 Happy Days!
Over 80s' Jokes	Yes to life! 365
Golf Jokes	The Mid-Life Disaster

EDITED BY HELEN EXLEY

Published in 2019 by Helen Exley ®LONDON in Great Britain.
Design, selection and arrangement © Helen Exley Creative Ltd 2019.
All the words by Stuart & Linda MacFarlane, Pamela Dugdale,
Jane Swan, Peter Gray, Pam Brown and Bill Stott copyright
© Helen Exley Creative Ltd 2019.
Cartoons copyright © Bill Stott 2019.
The moral rights of the authors have been asserted.

12 11 10 9 8 7 6 5 4 3 2 1

ISBN: 978-1-78485-233-7

FSC
MIX
Paper from
responsible sources
FSC® C081635
www.fsc.org

Helen Exley ®LONDON,
16 Chalk Hill, Watford, Herts WD19 4BG, UK
www.helenexley.com

Over 50's Jokes

CARTOONS BY BILL STOTT

Helen Exley

Middle age is when
you are sitting at home on
a Saturday night
and the telephone rings
and you hope it isn't for you.

OGDEN NASH

You know you're growing old when...
You still have the old spark,
but it takes more puffing to ignite.

RICHARD LEDERER

I try to take
one day at a time,
but sometimes
several days
attack me at once.

JENNIFER YANE

You can only hold your stomach in
for so many years.

BURT REYNOLDS

I'm too old to do things by half.

LOU REED

Fifty plus is when you suspect
you've flung your last fling
– but hope not.

PAM BROWN

At fifty, everyone has the face he deserves.

GEORGE ORWELL

The really frightening thing
about middle age
is the knowledge that
you'll grow out of it.

DORIS DAY

Every age has its springs which give
it movement; but man is always
the same. At ten years old he is led
by sweetmeats;
at twenty by a mistress;
at thirty by pleasure;
at forty by ambition;
at fifty by avarice;
after that what is left for him
to run after but wisdom?

JEAN-JACQUES ROUSSEAU

Well... you're only fifty once – right.

BILL STOTT

Apparently as you get older
you get wiser.
By that measure I must have an IQ
of over 200. It's just a pity
the Wi-Fi connection
to the Hard-Drive of my brain
seems to have been disconnected.

STUART & LINDA MACFARLANE

Look on the brighter
side of being bald.
At least you don't
have to wash your hair
any more.

DARA O'CONNELL

When you've reached a certain age
and think that a face-lift
or a trendy way of dressing
will make you feel twenty years younger,
remember – nothing
can fool a flight of stairs.

DENIS NORDEN

The first half of life
consists of the capacity
to enjoy without the chance,
the last half consists of the chance
without capacity.

MARK TWAIN

"What have you ever achieved
in your life,
except to fritter your time away?"
the lady asked her husband.
The husband replied,
"Don't worry, dear.
All our family are late developers."

Inside every older person
is a young person
wondering what happened.

JENNIFER YANE

People tend to gain in tolerance
and grow more generous-spirited
as they get older,
but on the other hand,
we often lose connectedness
and some degree of interest
in what's going on,
so our generosity is not all
that expensive to us.

ARTHUR RUBINSTEIN

The best thing about being
over the hill
is that now you can have some fun
and free-wheel down the other side.

ESTHER REES

You're not as young
as you used to be.
But you're not as old
as you're going to be.
So watch it!

IRISH TOAST

I'm the same weight
as when I was
twenty-five.
Unfortunately, at least thirty
per cent
of it's in one place...

BILL STOTT

I have long accepted
that the accumulation of years
means accepting certain changes.
On the downside,
my arms are now too short
for the eyesight.
On the upside,
the spreading of my *derrière*
means that I can check it in a mirror
without turning round.

SANDI TOKSVIG

Every morning and every evening
I do fifty push-ups.
Then I sleep in a desperate effort
to build my energy reserves back up.

STUART & LINDA MACFARLANE

The definition of an
Over-50's Swimmer:
someone who goes from the
50 metres backstroke
to the 50 minutes backache.

MIKE KNOWLES

Forty is the old
age of youth;
fifty the youth
of old age.

VICTOR HUGO

You know you're
fifty when your
address book is
full of people
you've forgotten.

PETER GRAY

Why do people say
"You're as young
as you feel?"
I'm only fifty
and I feel
like this already?

BILL STOTT

No Need to Worry

At the age of twenty we don't care
what the world thinks of us;
at thirty we worry about what it
thinks of us;
at fifty we discover that it isn't
thinking of us at all.

AUTHOR UNKNOWN

You know you're over fifty
when you hear things like,
"Take no notice, Dear –
I think grey hair looks
quite distinguished."

MIKE KNOWLES

My wife asked the question
that all men dread,
"Does my bum look big in this?"
Unfortunately I gave an honest reply.
My wife sulked for an hour then
came up with an ingenious method
so that I will never again think
her bum looks too big –
she put a paper bag over my head.

STUART & LINDA MACFARLANE

After thirty-five years of marriage Sam's wife died. At the end of a proper mourning period, Sam looked at himself and said, "Life is not over. I can go out and have some fun and perhaps meet a nice, younger woman and – who knows what?" Over an eighteen-month period Sam joined a gym to tone up, lost forty pounds, bought a toupee, had all his teeth capped, got a nose job, had a little tuck taken in his chin, grew a moustache, got contact lenses and bought a new youth-orientated wardrobe with elevator

shoes. Finally one day he was ready
to step out – he loved what he saw
in the mirror. Unfortunately, that night
Sam died and went to heaven,
whereupon he met God.

"God," said Sam, "I was a kind
and loving husband, a wonderful father
and grandfather, a charitable person,
and honest and hardworking in my
business. I was just about to start
a new life. Why did you do this?"
"Sam," replied God, "to tell you the truth,
I didn't recognise you."

FRED SHOENBERG

I don't believe in looking back.
I look ahead to what I'm going
to do tomorrow, next week, next month.
That gets my adrenaline going.
And these days getting my
adrenaline going is a little harder
than getting my car started.

GEORGE BURNS

When people
are old enough
to know better,
they're old enough
to do worse.

HESKETH PEARSON

Fifty is when you are pretty sure
that friends who say
"Don't you look well!"
mean Fat;
that friends who say
"I would never have known you!"
mean Old;
and that friends who say
"You'll be glad of that holiday!"
mean "Goodness. You look terrible."

PAM BROWN

Areas of most common complaints:

Starting difficulties
Poor performance
Exhaust problems
Misfiring
Loss of power
Chassis deterioration

FRED SHOENBERG

When you're a baby
you have skin like a peach.
When you get past fifty
your skin still looks like a fruit...
only this time it's a dried prune.

MIKE KNOWLES

I don't plan to grow old gracefully.
I plan to have face-lifts
until my ears meet.

RITA RUDNER

Five Steps to Longevity:
* Don't drink.
* Eat healthily.
* Don't smoke.
* Exercise frequently.
* Be totally miserable!

STUART & LINDA MACFARLANE

Age – you just wake up one morning,
and you got it.

JACKIE "MOMS" MABLEY

Turning fifty?
Laughter is the gift
that keeps you
in the present.

AUTHOR UNKNOWN

A helpful hint –
Always remember Diet Rules
– if no one sees you eat,
it has no calories
– snacks don't have any calories
if you eat them
quickly standing up
– salad makes you lose weight
no matter how much
dressing you put on it
– broken biscuits have no
calorific content
– if you drink diet Coke
with a Mars bar
they cancel each other out.

DAVID WASTWOOD

From birth to age eighteen,
a girl needs good parents;
from eighteen to thirty-five
she needs good looks;
from thirty-five to fifty-five
she needs a good personality;
and from fifty-five on
she needs cash.

SOPHIE TUCKER

The four stages of man are infancy, childhood, adolescence, and obsolescence.

ART LINKLETTER

"Don't worry. Be happy."
Yeah right!
What makes me happiest
is being thoroughly miserable
and making everyone else feel
miserable with my
apocalyptic predictions of
the terrible things
that are about to happen.

STUART & LINDA MACFARLANE

The prime of life
is that fleeting time between
green and over-ripe.

CULLEN HIGHTOWER

Rules to Live By in Middle Age

1. Never use catchy
philosophical phrases like:
"The best is yet to come" or
"We are about to enter the golden years."

2. Do not try to look 25. You won't.

3. Don't slow up on purpose.
Nature has its own braking system.

4. Middle age is mostly side effects
and behavioural deviations –
the heavy stuff is still out there.

FRED SHOENBERG

The only thing
I regret about my past
is the length of it.
If I had my life
to live again, I'd make
the same mistakes,
only sooner.

TALLULAH BANKHEAD

Face Lift: The classic beauty operation
whereby the surgeon makes an incision
under cover of the hairline,
pulls the facial skin taut,
puts in a tuck and cuts off the remains.
If performed too many times,
a patient could end up with his
tummy button up his nose.

CHRISTOPHER MATTHEW

Middle age starts
the morning you get up,
go to the bathroom,
look in the mirror and admit
that you are
who you are going to be.

FRED SHOENBERG

One of the saddest things of growing old is that you might have an illness that cannot be cured and the doctor might say, "We are very sorry, very, very, but we are going to have to put you down."

ALEX STANGER

Youth is a disease from which we all recover.

DOROTHY FULDHEIM

You are only young once, but you can be immature for a lifetime.

JOHN P. GRIER

Fifty's not the end of the world,
but you start to see it from there.

AUTHOR UNKNOWN

She could
very well pass for
forty-three,
in the dusk with
a light behind her.

W. S. GILBERT

Try to remember that,
with the exception of your parents
and your children,
most people
will consider you an adult.

FRED SHOENBERG

Middle age:
becoming like our parents while
fighting with our children.

ELLIOTT PRIEST

On my fiftieth birthday my wife gave me a superb birthday present. She let me win an argument.

AUTHOR UNKNOWN

Don't get me wrong –
a mountain bike at
fifty-plus is great.
Personally though –
I'd lose the lycra pants.

BILL STOTT

The first sign of age...
is when you go out into
the streets and recognise
for the first time how young
the policemen look.

SEYMOUR HICKS

You're not as spry as you were –
your mind is writing cheques
that your body can't cash!

JEFF BRIDGES

Middle age is...
when you start to say things like...
"In my day."

PAM BROWN

Fifty is when you begin to use the word Maturity a lot.

PAM BROWN

You know you're over fifty
when you prefer comedians
who use one liners.
That way you stand a good chance
of surviving long enough
to hear the punch line.

MIKE KNOWLES

One should never trust
a woman who tells one her real age.
A woman who would tell one
that would tell one anything.

OSCAR WILDE

The secret to a long life
is to stay busy,
get plenty of exercise,
and don't drink too much.
Then again,
don't drink too little.

HERMANN SMITH-JOHANNSON

We melted
all your candles
into one –
that way we got
fifty on one cake!

BILL STOTT

Middle age is
when everything
starts
to wear out,
fall out
or spread out.

AUTHOR UNKNOWN

Inside every slim,
beautiful woman,
is a fatter middle-aged woman
waiting to get out.

PAMELA DUGDALE

Middle age
is nature's way of showing
a sense of humour.

FRED SHOENBERG

Age is a question
of mind
over matter.
If you don't mind it
doesn't matter.

SATCHEL PAIGE

After thirty, a body

has a mind of its own.

BETTE MIDLER

It's hard to be devil-may-care
When there are pleats in your *derrière*.

JUDITH VIORST

The years that a woman
subtracts from her age
are not lost.
They are added to other women's.

DIANE DE POITIERS

I'm not fifty.
I'm just five perfect 10s!

AUTHOR UNKNOWN

A woman is as old as she looks before breakfast.

EDGAR WATSON HOWE

I refuse to admit that I am more than fifty-two, even if that does make my sons illegitimate.

LADY NANCY ASTOR

At middle age
you can no longer
plead ignorance
or innocence.
Now you're either
stupid or guilty.

FRED SHOENBERG

I cut my own hair.
I got sick of barbers
because they talk too much.
And too much of their talk
was about my hair falling out.

ROBERT FROST

Middle age is when
your hair starts turning
from grey to black.

JANE SWAN

Cheer up! The worst

s still to come!

PHILANDER CHASE JOHNSON

The best things in life
are free,
but it costs a lot of time
and money
before you find this out.

AUTHOR UNKNOWN

The Secret of Longevity

1. Don't run for a bus –
there'll always be another.

2. Never, ever touch fried food.

3. Stay out of a Ferrari or any other
small Italian car.

4. Eat fruit – a nectarine –
or even a rotten plum is good.

MEL BROOKS

You know you're over fifty
when you're still chasing the women,
you're still catching them,
and you still remember what to do...
but sometimes you start to wonder
why you bother.

MIKE KNOWLES

The secret of staying young
is to live honestly, eat slowly,
and lie about your age.

LUCILLE BALL

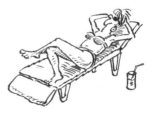

Middle age
is when it takes you
all night to do once
what once you used to do
all night.

KENNY EVERETT

One of the first signs
of getting old
is when your head makes dates
your body can't keep.

KEVIN GOLDSTEIN-JACKSON

There's one good thing
about being over fifty –
you don't need to sink
five pints before your
eyesight goes blurred.

MIKE KNOWLES

Fifty is the time
to get up and go
before
everything else does.

PAMELA DUGDALE

The trick is to grow up

They say life begins at fifty,
but so do lumbago, bad eyesight,
arthritis, and the habit of telling
the same story three times
to the same person.

AUTHOR UNKNOWN

without growing old.

FRANK LLOYD WRIGHT

One of the many things nobody
ever tells you about middle age
is that it's such a nice change
from being young.

DOROTHY CANFIELD FISHER

At my age
I don't care if
my mind starts
to wander –
just as long as it
comes back again.

MIKE KNOWLES

The denunciation of the young
is a necessary part of the hygiene
of older people,
and greatly assists the circulation
of the blood.

LOGAN PEARSALL SMITH

By the time you
get to fifty,
people expect you
to be mature,
responsible,
wise and dignified.
This is the time
to disillusion them.

PETER GRAY

Middle age is like
getting an invitation
to a great party
and then discovering
the party
was yesterday.

FRED SHOENBERG

The years between fifty
and seventy are the hardest.
You are always being asked
to do things,
and you are not yet
decrepit enough
to turn them down.

T. S. ELIOT

Don't criticize oldies
just realise they can't help it.
Being disillusioned
with the modern world
is our favourite hobby –
no, it's our responsibility.

NIELA ELIASON

When you are old
you do not have to
use your brains
so much because
they are a bit rusty.

KAREN EDWARDS

When you're over 50
you can still do all the things
you did when you were 17...
that's if you don't mind
making a complete prat of yourself.

MIKE KNOWLES

Looking fifty is grea

– if you're sixty.

LORD CALLAGHAN

The disadvantage of being old
is not looking as nice
as you did when you were young.
It is like looking at
a Before and After picture
but the other way round!

GINO MIELE

Experience
is the name
everyone gives
to their mistakes.

OSCAR WILDE

Middle age:
when you begin to exchange
your emotions for symptoms.

IRVIN S. COBB

You know you're getting
older when you wake up
with that morning-after feeling
and you didn't do anything
the night before.

S. L. P.

I complain that the years
fly past, but then I look in a mirror
and see that very few of them
actually got past.

ROBERT BRAULT

My wife said to me,
"I don't look fifty,
do I Darling?"
I said "Not any more."

BOB MONKHOUSE

Everything that goes up
must come down.
But there comes a time
when not everything
that's down can come up.

GEORGE BURNS

Middle age is when
instead of combing your hair,
you start "arranging" it.

HERBERT I. KAVET

The time to begin mos

hings is ten years ago.

I eat healthy foods
that help keep my brain young:
blueberries, salmon and eggs.
Recently I very nearly
ate some broccoli!

STUART & LINDA MACFARLANE

Blepharoplasty:
The operation that takes away
the bags under your eyes,
the better to allow them to open
in stunned belief at the subsequent bill.
Chemical Peel:
a hair– (not to say skin-)
raising method of burning the wrinkles
off the face with strong chemicals,
or possibly with a rotating wire brush.
For those who fancy a complexion
like a brick wall.

CHRISTOPHER MATTHEW

You know you're
over fifty when
some joker says you
need a hurricane
to blow out the candles
on your
birthday cake.

MIKE KNOWLES

After fifty,
feeling fit
is a sure sign
that something is
drastically wrong.

STUART & LINDA MACFARLANE

Middle age
is when
we can do just
as much as ever
but would
rather not.

DR. LAURENCE J. PETER

You're over fifty
when the spirit's willing –
but the flesh is exhausted.

PAM BROWN

Last night the police raided
one of these over 50's raves
and confiscated some of the things
they take to keep going:
three elasticated stockings,
a quantity of multivitamin tablets,
and a zimmer frame.

MIKE KNOWLES

Middle age is when you
find out where the action is
so you can go someplace else.

PATRICIA PENTON LEIMBACH

I act like a 10 year old.
I dress like a 20 year old.
I think like a 30 year old.
Oh!!! If only I looked
like a 40 year old.

STUART & LINDA MACFARLANE

As you move into a new decade
it's all right to feel
optimistic about the years ahead.
You can cry about them later
when the harsh reality
becomes apparent.

STUART & LINDA MACFARLANE

You know you're getting older
when you do the crossword puzzle
in ink because you can't read
the answers in pencil.

AUTHOR UNKNOWN

Middle age
is when anything
new you feel
is most likely
to be a symptom.

DR. LAURENCE J. PETER

...you wake up one morning
and there's a spot on your face,
or the back of your hand,
that you never saw before
and you're sure it's cancer.
Your eyesight
has been getting steadily worse:
brain tumour.
A little gas: heart attack.
Pretty soon you're showing
symptoms of whatever ailment
you saw on television
the night before.
I call it '*disease du jour.*'

FRED SHOENBERG

I make no attempt to
remember my age –
that would seem so calculating.
Instead I tell everyone
that I am forty-nine.
There is something beautiful
about forty-nine as an age –
and I see no reason why any lady
should ever exceed it.

STUART & LINDA MACFARLANE

You're over the hill
when you feel like
the morning after
and you can swear
you haven't been anywhere.

DR. LAURENCE J. PETER

Middle age is when you would do
anything to feel better except
give up what's hurting you.

HERBERT V. PROCHNOW AND
HERBERT V. PROCHNOW JNR.

Youth is a
wonderful thing.
It's such a pity
it's wasted
on the young.

AUTHOR UNKNOWN

The idea is to die young

as late as possible.

ASHLEY MONTAGUE

For the last six months
I have been regularly buying
an expensive rejuvenation cream
on an internet site.
It claims that it will make you
look like a teenager again.
In a way it worked –
after buying it for six months
I feel as poor as I did
when I was a student.

STUART & LINDA MACFARLANE

My wife's
come up with
this great cure
for wrinkles –
she just
irons my face.

MIKE KNOWLES

They say
that when you're
over fifty
one of the
first things
to go is your…
now what
was I saying?

ANGUS WALKER

Nothing ages you faster
than trying to prove
you're still as young as ever.

E. C. MCKENZIE

The fact is that getting
your hair dyed
and having facial
beauty treatment
will make you look
ten years older.

STUART & LINDA MACFARLANE

Old age
is when you can't
remember what
you never forget.

AUTHOR UNKNOWN

The best thing
about getting old is that
all those things
you couldn't have
when you were young
you no longer want.

L. S. MCCANDLESS

"For a fifty year old,
you're in terrible shape."
"Nonsense. I demand
a second opinion."
"Ok you're ugly too."

BILL STOTT

Man is old when he begins
to hide his age;
woman,
when she begins to tell hers.

OSCAR WILDE

I was telling, my son
about the advantages
of being over fifty.
"As you get older," I said,
"you get wiser."
He looked at me and replied,
"In that case
you must be a genius."

ANGUS WALKER

I seem to have become expert
in napping.
I am able to nap on a bus,
on a train, in the bath – anywhere.
The only time I have difficulty
napping is at night –
I suffer dreadfully with insomnia.

STUART & LINDA MACFARLANE

Middle age is the time
when a man is always thinking
that in a week or two
he will feel just as good as ever.

DON MARQUIS

Fifty is when people
expect you to
have answers.
Just as you are
beginning to doubt
if there are any.

PAMELA DUGDALE

You know you're over fifty
when the doctor tells you
you've reached that point in your life
when hard work can kill you.

MIKE KNOWLES

The older we get, the

better we used to be.

JOHN MCENROE

Don't worry about it –
you don't look a day over fifty.
Mind you, you always were
a mature fifty.

BILL STOTT

"The fuss you made of that minx,"
complained the middle-aged
wife to her husband.
"Are you already in your
second childhood?"
"Not yet," the husband's eyes
continued to twinkle.
"But perhaps I'm just starting
on my second adolescence!"

GORDON WILLIAMS

If you can't be
a good example,
then you'll just
have to be a
horrible warning.

CATHERINE AIRD

No woman
should be quite
accurate
about her age.
It looks so
calculating.

OSCAR WILDE

Age seldom arrives smoothly
or quickly. It's more often
a succession of jerks.

JEAN RHYS

When you have a birthday
and you are middle aged
your friends all clink their glasses
and cheer and it gives you
a headache.

PHILLIP BROOKE

Take my advice –
it's best to ignore
your birthday –
unless you want it to
grow old and rusty.

ESTHER REES

Life moves pretty fast;
if you don't stop and look around
every once in a while,
you could miss it.

MATTHEW BRODERICK

Experience. The wisdom
that enables us to recognize
in an undesirable old
acquaintance the folly that
we have already embraced.

AMBROSE BIERCE

Every time I try
to take out a new lease on life,
the landlord raises the rent.

ASHLEIGH BRILLIANT

Now I'm over fifty
my doctor says I should go out
and get more fresh
air and exercise.
I said, "All right.
I'll drive with
the car window open."

ANGUS WALKER

Life would be infinitely happier
if we could only be born
at the age of eighty and gradually
approach eighteen.

MARK TWAIN

Fifty is the time between
Well-preserved and Smart.
Hang on to Elegance.

PAMELA DUGDALE

The advantage
of exercising
every day is
that you
die healthier.

AUTHOR UNKNOWN

You know you are getting old when people tell you how good you look.

ALAN KING

Middle age occurs when you are too young to take up golf and too old to rush up to the net.

FRANKLIN P. ADAMS

Five Signs of Growing Older

1. When you look at the menu
before you look at the waitress.

2. When you wait for a crowded escalator
rather than walk up the empty stairs.

3. When an 8 looks like a 3 and
a 3 like an 8.

4. When you would rather sit on the beach
than go in the water.

5. When you leave a good party early
because you don't want to feel bad
the next day.

AUTHOR UNKNOWN

Age is a very high price

When you are old
your body creaks
and your knees knock
and your teeth
fall out.

ADRIAN TYDD

to pay for maturity.

TOM STOPPARD

One trouble with growing older
is that it gets progressively tougher
to find a famous historical figure
who didn't amount to much
when he was your age.

BILL VAUGHAN

You know you're fifty
when being
comfortable outweighs
practically
everything else.

PAMELA DUGDALE

Old age is like everything else.
To make a success of it
you've got to start young.

FRED ASTAIRE

You grow up the day
you have your first real laugh
at yourself.

ETHEL BARRYMORE

I have everything now I had
twenty years ago –
except now it's all lower.

GYPSY ROSE LEE

There is only one thing
wrong with the
younger generation –
a lot of us don't
belong to it anymore.

BERNARD M. BARUCH

Middle age is when
you're willing to get up
and give your seat
to a lady – and can't.

SAMMY KAY

"He was a beautiful child...
unfortunately he peaked at twelve."

BILL STOTT

Youth would be an ideal state if it came a little later in life.

LORD HERBERT ASQUITH

My husband never chases
another women.
He's too fine, too decent, too old!

GRACIE ALLEN

I was getting dressed
and a peeping tom
looked in the window,
took a look and pulled down
the shade.

JOAN RIVERS

Do you know you get
white hair from worrying
about your wrinkles.

PAM BROWN

A sure sign of middle age
is that, although we love seeing
a "10" on the beach,
we're willing to settle for two "5's."

FRED SHOENBERG

Experience is a good teacher, but she sends in terrific bills.

MINNA ANTRIM

You know you're growing older
when you'd pay good money
to be strip-searched.

RICHARD LEDERER

When I was young,
I was told:
"You'll see when
you're fifty."
I am fifty and
I haven't seen a thing.

ERIK SATIE

He was over fifty and
he looked it. In fact his face
was that hard and wrinkled
the neighbours sharpened
their knives on it.

MIKE KNOWLES

You are fifty when you're still
not sure about gadgets everyone else
knows how to work.

PAM BROWN

When we're young we want to
change the world. When we're older
we want to change the young.

AUTHOR UNKNOWN

You're over fifty
when your clothes
no longer fit
and it's you who needs
the alterations.

EARL WILSON

Oh come on –
being fifty's
not so bad.
It's not good,
but it's not so bad...

BILL STOTT

Don't worry
about avoiding temptation.
As you grow older,
it will avoid you.

JOEY ADAMS

Old age is when candlelit dinners
are no longer romantic because
you can't read the menu.

CINDY PATTERSON

The older one grows,
the more one likes indecency.

VIRGINIA WOOLF

"Okay – you're the same weight as you were at thirty-five. You were a chubby thirty-five."

BILL STOTT

Certain connections just seem
to be beyond me at this age.
For example, if someone calls me
on the telephone and says,
"Can you meet me at
the Seven-Eleven at eight?"
I show up at
the Five-and-Ten at nine.

BILL COSBY

I'm definitely not ageing,
just marinating.

AUTHOR UNKNOWN

When women
pass thirty,
they first forget
their age;
when fifty,
they forget
that they ever
remembered it.

NINON DE L'ENCLOS

"What do you mean –
I look younger than Carol O'Brien?
Carol O'Brien is fifty-six."

BILL STOTT

I'm getting to an age
when I can only enjoy the last
sport left. It is called hunting
for your spectacles.

LORD GREY OF FALLODEN

You know you're getting older
when you can't get
your rocking chair started.

AUTHOR UNKNOWN

When you're over fifty, you suddenly become appalled by the way that modern mirrors distort the reflection.

PETER GRAY

I'm at an age
where my back
goes out
more than I do.

PHYLLIS DILLER

Middle age is…
when you need to have a rest
after tying your shoelaces.

MIKE KNOWLES

How come at a class reunion
you feel so much younger
than everybody else looks?

AUTHOR UNKNOWN

Over fifty is when
keeping your hair on means
wearing a toupée.

PAM BROWN

Age is not important unless you're a cheese.

HELEN HAYES

Everything slows down with age,
except the time it takes cake
and ice cream to reach your hips.

JOHN WAGNER

You know you're fifty when you're hurrying for a train – and people out for a lazy stroll pass you at speed.

PETER GRAY

If you can't laugh at your wrinkles and aches, you've got to scream.

KATHY LETTE

You know you're
getting older
when you look
forward to a dull
evening in.

AUTHOR UNKNOWN

It is better to wea

You know you're
getting old
when the candles
cost more
than the cake.

BOB HOPE

ut than rust out.

RICHARD CUMBERLAND

I exercise every morning without fail.
Up, down! Up, down!
And then the other eyelid.

ANTHONY HOPKINS